MANAGING THE MONEY

Athlete Contracts and Salary Caps

By Tom Schad

SportsZone
An Imprint of Abdo Publishing
abdobooks.com

abdobooks.com

Published by Abdo Publishing, a division of ABDO, PO Box 398166, Minneapolis, Minnesota 55439.

Printed in the United States of America, North Mankato, Minnesota.
102025
012026

THIS BOOK CONTAINS RECYCLED MATERIALS

Cover Photo: Mary DeCicco/Major League Baseball Photos/Getty Images
Interior Photos: Greg Fiume/Getty Images Sport/Getty Images, 1, 23; Rich Graessle/Icon Sportswire, 3, 26; Jamie Squire/Getty Images Sport/Getty Images, 4–5; Cindy Ord/Getty Images for Leigh Steinberg/Getty Images Entertainment/Getty Images, 6; Rich Graessle/Icon Sportswire/Getty Images, 7; Andy Kuno/San Francisco Giants/Getty Images Sport/Getty Images, 8–9; David Eulitt/Getty Images Sport/Getty Images, 11; Mike Buscher/Cal Sport Media/Alamy Live News/Alamy, 12, 45; Brett Deering/Getty Images Sport/Getty Images, 14–15; Fernando Medina/NBAE/National Basketball Association/Getty Images, 17; Richard Pelham/Getty Images Sport/Getty Images, 18; Cameron Browne/NBAE/National Basketball Association/Getty Images, 20; David Sherman/NBAE/National Basketball Association/Getty Images, 22–23; Tim Warner/Getty Images Sport/Getty Images, 24–25; Rob Leiter/Major League Baseball/Getty Images, 28–29; Shaun Botterill/Getty Images Sport/Getty Images, 31; Ronald C. Modra/Getty Images Sport/Getty Images, 32–33; George Gojkovich/Getty Images Sport/Getty Images, 35; Harry How/Getty Images Sport/Getty Images, 36–37; David Berding/Getty Images Sport/Getty Images, 39, 47; Mike Ehrmann/Getty Images Sport/Getty Images, 40–41; Elsa/Getty Images Sport/Getty Images, 42–43

Editor: Christa Kelly
Series Designer: Maggie Villaume

Library of Congress Control Number: 2025939226

Publisher's Cataloging-in-Publication Data

Names: Schad, Tom, author.
Title: Managing the money: athlete contracts and salary caps / by Tom Schad
Description: Minneapolis, Minnesota: Abdo Publishing, 2026 | Series: The business of sports | Includes online resources and index.
Identifiers: ISBN 9781098298265 (lib. bdg.) | ISBN 9798384932062 (ebook)
Subjects: LCSH: Sports--Juvenile literature. | Sports sponsorship--Juvenile literature. | Professional sports contracts--Juvenile literature. | Sports--Economic aspects--Juvenile literature. | Money managers (Investment advisors)--Juvenile literature. | Sports in popular culture--Juvenile literature.
Classification: DDC 338.43796--dc23

TABLE OF CONTENTS

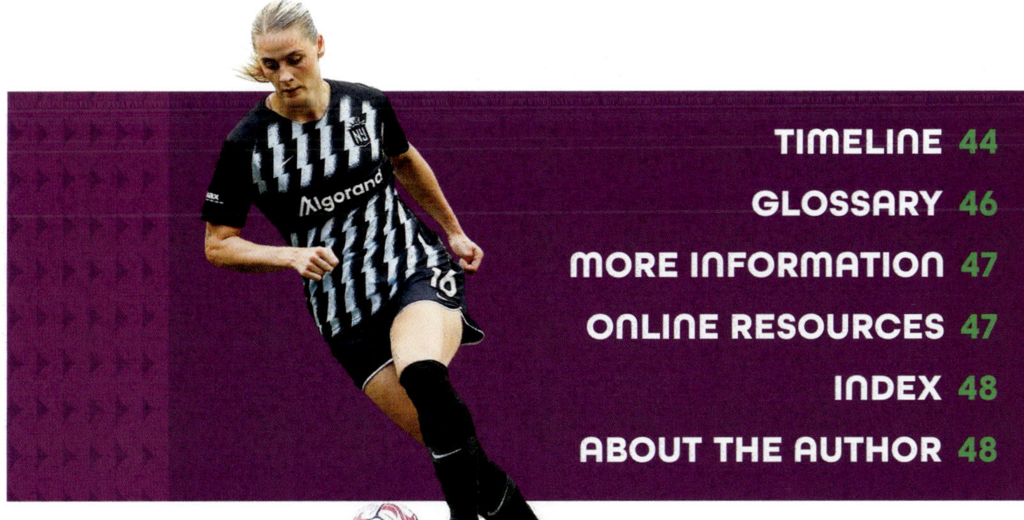

NFL
CHAMPS!
SUPER BOWL
CHAMPIONS
KC

CHAPTER ONE

MAKING MILLIONS

Kansas City Chiefs quarterback Patrick Mahomes had already been one of the best players in the National Football League (NFL). But on February 2, 2020, he became a star. At Super Bowl LIV in Miami, Mahomes led the Chiefs on three touchdown drives in the fourth quarter to cap a come-from-behind 31–20 victory over the San Francisco 49ers.

The win gave Mahomes, who was just 24 years old, his first Super Bowl ring. It also gave Kansas City its first championship in 50 years. After the game, Mahomes celebrated with his teammates. He hoisted the Vince Lombardi Trophy over his head as confetti swirled around him. The next day, he went to Florida's Walt Disney World and paraded through Magic Kingdom with Mickey Mouse.

Patrick Mahomes led the Kansas City Chiefs to victory in Super Bowl LIV in just his third NFL season.

Chris Cabott, *left*, and Leigh Steinberg, *right*, worked together at Steinberg Sports & Entertainment before parting ways in 2023.

Meanwhile, behind the scenes, Mahomes's agents Chris Cabott and Leigh Steinberg were hard at work. For months, they had been talking with the Chiefs about the star quarterback's contract. A contract is a promise between an athlete and a team or the people who are organizing a sport. Mahomes's current contract promised he would play for the Chiefs. In exchange, the Chiefs paid Mahomes a certain amount of money. But his contract was nearly over. His agents were working on a new contract. Their goal was to get Mahomes more money. Winning a Super Bowl gave them leverage.

Later that summer, as Mahomes and the team continued to celebrate their Super Bowl championship, the agents' plan paid off. Mahomes, the Super Bowl Most Valuable Player, signed a new contract worth $450 million over 10 years. It was the biggest contract in American sports and one of the longest contracts in NFL history.

Some NFL fans thought Mahomes was making a mistake by signing such a long contract so early in his career. What if he led the Chiefs to more Super Bowl wins? Wouldn't he be worth more money than what was in his contract?

Mahomes saw it differently. The 10-year contract meant he would stay in Kansas City for all, or almost all, of his NFL career.

Mahomes earned his first NFL Most Valuable Player Award in 2018.

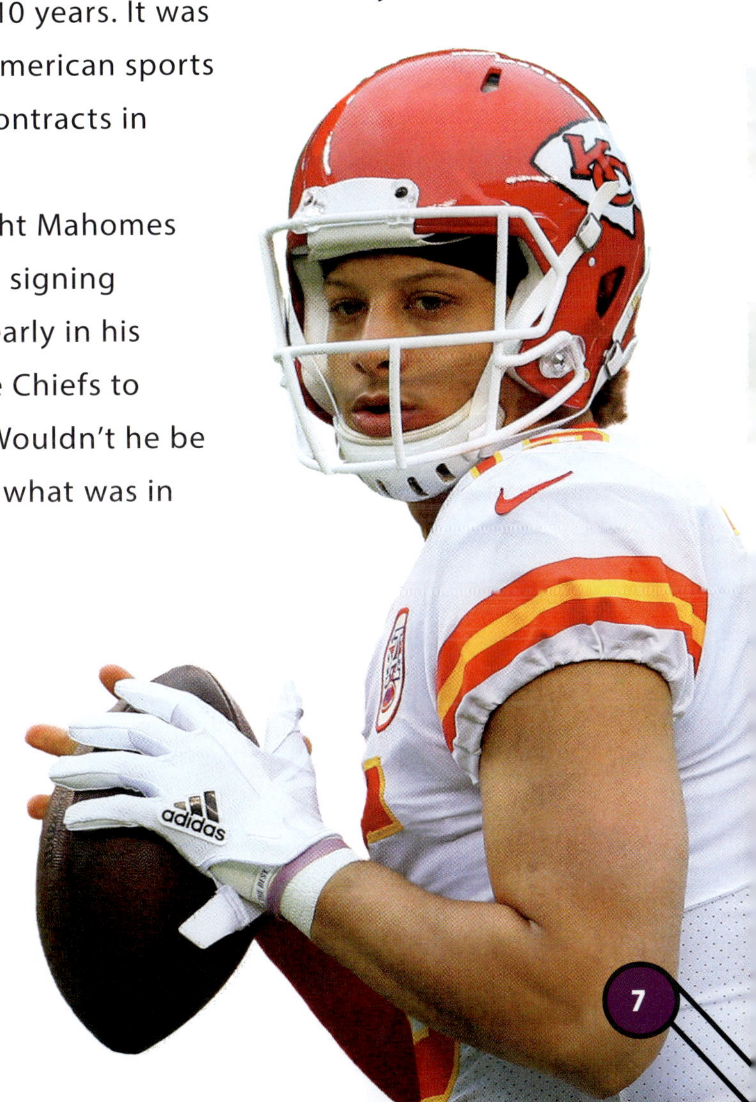

And by making a little bit less money, he would give the Chiefs more money to spend on other players. He hoped this would make the team better and help the Chiefs win more Super Bowls.

"The best thing that happened was the Chiefs and my team, we went in with an open mind," Mahomes told a reporter later that summer. "We tried to figure out what was not only best for me and my family, but also what was best for the team moving forward."

The Foundation of Sports

Professional sports teams make contracts every year. From the NFL and the National Basketball Association (NBA) to individual sports such as boxing and golf, contracts are at the foundation of sports. Athletes in team sports sign contracts to promise that they will practice, play in games, and always try their hardest to win. In return, teams promise to pay the athletes certain amounts of money. Athletes in individual sports sign contracts promising to attend sporting events.

Athletes often have help negotiating their contracts.

GIGANTES
ORACLE PARK
GIANTS

Each contract is a little bit different. The details of a contract can vary depending on the people, team, and league or sporting event involved. Some contracts are simple, such as those for track-and-field events. These contracts promise athletes an appearance fee. An appearance fee is money for showing up to an event and competing. The same amount of money is paid whether the athlete wins or loses.

Other contracts are more complicated. Sometimes money is paid all at once. Other times it is paid over a long period of time. Some contracts reward athletes with a bonus for hitting specific benchmarks. An NFL quarterback might get a bonus for throwing a certain number of touchdown passes. An NBA player might get a bonus for averaging a certain number of rebounds. Contracts may also penalize athletes for bad behavior away from the field or court.

In individual sports, there is no cap on how much money an athlete can make in a contract. But in some sports leagues, there is a limit on how much money each team can spend paying its players. This is called a salary cap.

Salary caps are supposed to give each team in the league a fair chance to win by making sure that no one team can spend more money than the others. However, this cap can also make negotiating contracts difficult. Teams must carefully balance each player's contract.

Chris Jones began his NFL career with the Chiefs in 2016.

When Mahomes signed his contract in 2020 after leading the Chiefs to the Super Bowl, he knew that one of his teammates, defensive lineman Chris Jones, also wanted a new contract. The Chiefs had to find a way to give both players more money without going over the salary cap for the season. Failing to do so would mean risking losing one of the players. In the end, Mahomes agreed to take only a small part of his $450 million in the first few years of his deal. That gave the

In 2025, the Chiefs restructured both Mahomes's and Jones's contracts to avoid going over the team's salary cap. This means the players will be paid less now but get more money later.

Chiefs some room to offer Jones a four-year contract worth $85 million.

"When Pat's deal got done, Pat texted me and said, 'Let's get this thing done. I left some (money) on the table, let's get this thing done,'" Jones recalls. "And that's when I had the security that me and the Chiefs were going to work something out."

Together, Mahomes and Jones helped lead the Chiefs to two more Super Bowl victories over the next four years. But it doesn't always work out that way. Sometimes a team runs out of money and has to cut a player. A team may also have to trade a player to another team in exchange for a cheaper player, money, or a better pick in a future draft.

Each athlete and team has to make tough choices when drawing up contracts. Teams and athletes often disagree about the best choices to make. But both groups understand that contracts are essential to creating strong teams. While Super Bowl championships are won on the field by players like Mahomes, a winning season starts with promises on paper.

THE MOST EXPENSIVE CONTRACTS IN SPORTS

When Patrick Mahomes signed his $450 million contract in 2020, the deal was the most expensive contract in the history of American professional sports. But it didn't stay that way for long. In 2023, baseball star Shohei Ohtani signed a free-agent contract with the Los Angeles Dodgers. It was worth a whopping $700 million over 10 years. The next year, Juan Soto made history with a 15-year, $765 million contract with the New York Mets.

OKLAHOMA
11
XII
OU

CHAPTER TWO

HOW ATHLETES GET PAID

Point guard Trae Young was considered one of the best high school basketball players in the country. When he went to the University of Oklahoma, he quickly became one of the best players at the collegiate level. By the time he made it to the 2018 NBA Draft, all eyes were on Young.

The Dallas Mavericks took Young with the fifth pick in the NBA Draft. Then they traded him to the Atlanta Hawks. Young signed a four-year contract with the Hawks worth more than $26 million.

It was a life-changing amount of money for a 19-year-old. Young celebrated by buying his mom a new car. "Just everything she's helped me

Trae Young played for the University of Oklahoma for only one season.

with and been through, the way she's handled herself, I wanted to do something special for her," Young said.

When Young signed his first contract, he officially became a professional athlete. Playing his sport was no longer a hobby. It was his job. Across the world of sports, this is how many athletes are introduced to contracts. They sign their first deals when they join their first professional team. By signing contracts, athletes such as Young are taking on new responsibilities. And in the biggest leagues, signing a contract also comes with a lot of money.

What's in a Contract?

For athletes, money is often the most important part of each contract. A contract dictates how much an athlete will be paid. It also clarifies when the athlete will be paid. Some contracts outline conditions that can lead to athletes being paid more or less.

Individual sports often have the simplest contracts. In these contracts, an athlete's pay is often tied to a single event. The athlete is paid a certain amount for participating in a game, tournament, or race. Individual athletes might sign several contracts each year.

Some athletes sign contracts that promise money based on the athletes' performance. They get more money for winning

In 2021, Young signed a five-year extension with the Atlanta Hawks for more than $215 million.

ATLANTA
11
HAWKS

SEASON

or scoring well. In sports such as boxing, a contract can even link an athlete's pay to the success of the event. For example, boxers' pay can depend in part on how many fans buy tickets to their fight or pay to watch it on TV.

Contracts are often more complex for athletes participating in team sports. Each contract ties an athlete to a certain team. The contract lasts for a certain period of time. In exchange, the athlete receives the amount of money agreed upon in the contract.

In team sports, an athlete's pay is usually broken down into two parts. These parts are the athlete's base salary and the available bonuses. Base salary is what the athlete is paid for being part of the team. It is generally paid over a period of time. Bonuses are extra earnings. They are usually paid in big chunks. An athlete might receive a bonus for their performance. Bonuses can also be given as annual rewards. A contract may offer a big up-front payment in the form of a signing bonus. Athletes can also get roster bonuses for being on the team at the start of a season.

Leagues with salary caps typically set a minimum and maximum amount that players can be paid per year. This amount can be impacted by how long an athlete has been in a league. In the NBA, rookies get a certain percentage of a team's overall salary cap. The percentage is determined by

Since turning professional in 2013, heavyweight boxer Anthony Joshua has earned more than $250 million.

Deandre Ayton played for the Phoenix Suns from 2018 to 2023 before moving to the Portland Trail Blazers.

which place they were picked in the draft. For example, Young was chosen fifth in his draft. He signed a $26 million contract. Fellow rookie Deandre Ayton was chosen first. His contract was worth more than $40 million.

The rules that limit rookie salaries also limit the lengths of contracts. In the NBA, a rookie deal can't be more than four years long. This means after four years, a player can negotiate a new deal. In Young's case, his new contract was worth $207 million. That's more than seven times as much as his rookie contract. It was the maximum amount he could be paid under NBA rules.

Contracts also outline what is expected of athletes. A contract explains what happens if the athlete gets hurt or breaks a team rule. Contracts also describe the ways athletes can end their contracts or move to different teams.

For some athletes, the freedom in a contract can be as important as the money. Many star athletes want to be able to decide which teams they play for and who they play with. To achieve this, an agent can negotiate something called an opt-out clause. This clause gives an athlete a window in which they can leave a team without penalty. If an athlete opts out, they can sign with any team in free agency.

The no-trade clause is another tool athletes can use to take control of their careers. The clause can prevent an athlete from being traded to another team. The clause

TREVOR ARIZA'S TRADES

Trading players is an inevitable part of professional sports. But for former NBA forward Trevor Ariza, the moves between teams got a little crazy. Ariza is believed to be the most traded player in league history. Over the course of his 18-year career, he played for 12 different teams and was part of 11 trades. He was even traded three times in a span of just six days during the 2020–21 season.

can also limit which teams the athlete can be traded to.

When athletes are traded, their contracts remain in place. They continue to be paid the same amount of money they were paid under their previous teams. They also have to follow the same rules. However, a trade can be a good chance for an athlete to rework their deal. Contracts can be changed with the consent of both parties. When an athlete is traded, the new team will sometimes offer the athlete more money. They might also negotiate a shorter or longer contract.

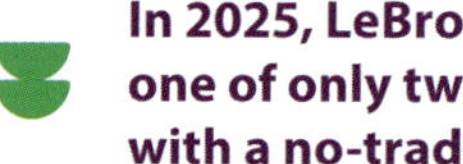

In 2025, LeBron James was one of only two NBA players with a no-trade clause.

CASE STUDY

CAITLIN CLARK

When Caitlin Clark joined the Women's National Basketball Association (WNBA) in 2024, she was already among the biggest names in women's basketball. Fans flocked to Indiana Fever games to see her play. But because of the limits in the league's rookie pay scale, her salary during her rookie year was tiny. She made just $78,000.

Clark, however, is proof that many athletes don't rely only on the money from their playing contracts. In addition to her WNBA deal, she signed a string of endorsement deals with big companies, including Gatorade and Nike. Those deals paid her millions. In fact, her salary with the Fever made up less than 1 percent of the $11 million she earned in 2024.

Clark is not alone. International soccer superstar Lionel Messi made $70 million in endorsements, compared to $20 million in salary from Inter Miami of Major League Soccer (MLS). And for athletes in Olympic sports, such as gymnast Simone Biles and sprinter Sydney McLaughlin-Levrone, endorsement deals provide the big-money paychecks that their sports cannot.

Caitlin Clark was named WNBA Rookie of the Year in 2024.

Rakuten
GOLDEN
30
WARRIORS

CHAPTER THREE

HOW TEAMS AND LEAGUES MANAGE MONEY

Managing contracts can be complicated. Each contract is part of a bigger financial puzzle. Executives spend a lot of time and money getting the pieces to fit together. Each team's goal is to spend the money necessary to have a good team while also following their league's salary rules.

Each league has its own salary rules. Some leagues have hard salary caps. A hard salary cap is a strict limit on how much money a team can spend on its players during a season. The NFL, the WNBA, MLS, the National Hockey League (NHL), and the National Women's Soccer League (NWSL) all have hard salary caps.

Golden State Warriors guard Stephen Curry was the NBA's highest-paid player in 2024–25, earning more than $55 million.

In 2025, the NWSL's salary cap was $3.3 million.

The size of a league's salary cap is usually determined by how much money the league brings in. This means that teams in more popular leagues generally have more money to spend. Each NHL team had a salary cap of $88 million in 2025. But the NFL is more popular. Each NFL team had a salary cap of $279 million.

Other leagues have soft caps. The NBA is one such league. While hard salary caps can't be exceeded, soft caps are flexible. In certain situations, a team can go above the salary cap number to pay a player. However, that team will have to pay a luxury tax. This is a punishment for overspending. These taxes encourage teams to stay below their salary caps.

Major League Baseball (MLB) has a soft salary cap. But the richest teams routinely ignore it. In 2024, MLB owners paid a whopping $311 million in luxury taxes. The Los Angeles Dodgers and New York Mets went especially far over their salary caps. Each team had a luxury tax of more than $97 million.

Among major US sports leagues, MLB has the least strict rules about paying players. This helps explain why some baseball players are among the highest-paid athletes in all of American sports. MLB rules also enable the richest teams to buy the best players. Critics say this makes the league predictable. The teams that spend the most money are usually the most likely to win.

Behind the Scenes

Professional sports teams have owners. The owners pay the teams' bills. And almost every owner hires a general manager to put together their team. General managers make trades, draft players, and decide who will and won't make the team.

Many teams also hire salary cap experts. A salary cap expert is tasked with managing a team's spending. These experts look for creative ways to bend the rules and stay under the salary cap. They determine not only where a team's money is spent but also how and when. For example, a salary cap expert may recommend that a team pays a player more or less in certain seasons, rather than the same amount every year.

Each league monitors the spending of its teams to ensure that nobody breaks the rules. This keeps the leagues fair. It also makes sure no team is at risk of running out of money.

The Union of European Football Associations (UEFA) governs soccer in Europe. Among its roles is monitoring spending across the continent's various leagues. UEFA has rules that compare a team's spending with its revenue. These financial fair-play rules force teams to spend only what they make over a period of three years. If a team

The Los Angeles Dodgers spent more than $321 million in 2025, far over MLB's $241 million soft salary cap.

LA
Dodgers
18

CASE STUDY
DAVID BECKHAM

In 2006, MLS wanted to convince Real Madrid midfielder David Beckham, one of the best soccer players in the world, to join its league. However, the league's salary cap was relatively low. MLS didn't have a team that could afford Beckham's salary.

The league found a creative solution. It was informally called the Beckham Rule. MLS began allowing its teams to sign one player who would not count toward the team's salary cap. This paved the way for the Los Angeles Galaxy to offer Beckham a contract in 2007 worth $6.5 million per year. That's more than three times higher than the league's salary cap that year.

Beckham's deal had a massive impact on MLS. His popularity drew new fans and millions of dollars in new revenue to the sport. There was so much excitement around the league that it started adding new teams. And the league's new rule helped MLS attract more big names from European soccer. MLS eventually expanded the rule. Now teams can sign three players who do not count toward the team's salary cap.

The deal also worked out well for Beckham. On top of his $6.5 million annual salary, his contract allowed him to receive a portion of the money that the Galaxy generated by selling jerseys and tickets. The contract also gave him a future opportunity to purchase an MLS team for $25 million. Beckham is now a co-owner of Inter Miami.

overspends in one season, it must spend less the next year to make up for it.

These financial regulations are just one way in which European soccer differs from American sports leagues such as the NFL and WNBA. In major European soccer leagues, such as England's Premier League, teams do not trade with one another. Instead, they buy and sell player contracts. This means teams can add players without giving up any of their own.

NAOMI GIRMA

Women's sports are exploding in popularity. This is putting more money in these sports. In 2025, English soccer team Chelsea paid the NWSL's San Diego Wave $1.1 million for the rights to Naomi Girma. That made the American defender the first million-dollar player in women's soccer. She is also reportedly one of the highest paid players in the Women's Super League.

In contrast, American sports leagues trade players frequently. Trading players is one way leagues can manage contracts. Sometimes a team will trade to get a player who is a better fit. Other times a team will trade a player to get rid of a contract. If a player is making a lot of money but not performing well, the team could view their contract as a bad deal.

David Beckham played for the Los Angeles Galaxy from 2007 to 2012.

NEW YORK

CHAPTER FOUR

CREATIVE CONTRACT SOLUTIONS

Outfielder Bobby Bonilla had once been among the highest-paid players in baseball. But after a dismal performance during the 1999 season, the New York Mets wanted out. The Mets decided to cut Bonilla from the team even though he still had $5.9 million left on his contract.

Bonilla offered the Mets a deal. The team could pay him all of the money they owed him in one chunk, or they could wait until 2011 to start paying him, spreading out the payments over 25 years. In that case, they would have to pay interest. It would mean paying Bonilla a total of about $30 million instead of $5.9 million.

Bobby Bonilla played in MLB from 1986 to 2001, including five seasons with the New York Mets.

Mets owner Fred Wilpon liked this idea. He thought the team could actually save money by paying Bonilla a little bit of money over a long time. By investing Bonilla's $5.9 million in the stock market, Wilpon believed he could make more than enough money to cover the interest Bonilla would be owed. Waiting to pay would also buy the Mets some time.

Bonilla didn't mind waiting for his payout. Now, he gets a little more than $1 million on the same date each year even though he's retired. Mets fans have started referring to that date, July 1, as Bobby Bonilla Day.

Bonilla's pay arrangement is a good example of a deferral. This is when a team and an athlete agree to postpone, or defer, the payment of money the athlete has earned. In baseball, Bonilla's deal helped revolutionize the way that teams approach contracts. While Bonilla's deferral came at the end of his time with the Mets, many teams now offer deferrals when they sign new players.

In 2023, baseball player Shohei Ohtani took the idea of a deferral to a new level. He signed a 10-year, $700 million contract with the Los Angeles Dodgers. But he will actually get only $20 million from the Dodgers over those 10 years. The other $680 million will be paid over the next 10 years. This means Ohtani will get $68 million per year after his contract ends.

Before playing for the Mets, Bonilla spent six seasons with the Pittsburgh Pirates.

“I have some clients who like [deferrals], and others who don’t,” Ohtani’s agent, Nez Balelo, told a reporter. “Some want to be aggressive with their money, saying ‘What if I can get that money up front and invest it properly?’ While others like having that guaranteed money coming in every year after they retire.”

Bonuses and Guarantees

A deferral is just one of the many creative solutions that athletes and teams use in contracts. Teams can pay a lot of money all at once as a signing bonus. Or they can pay a little bit over a long period of time. Everyone has a different opinion about what makes a contract appealing.

When looking for creative solutions, both teams and players are trying to protect themselves. An athlete typically wants to guarantee as much money as possible while also being careful not to limit future earning potential. Some players like

At the time of signing in 2023, Shohei Ohtani’s 10-year, $700 million contract was the biggest contract in baseball history.

LA
Dodgers

long contracts. A long contract ensures the athlete continues to make money even if they suffer a career-ending injury. But it can also lock a player into a bad situation. A long contract can also limit how much money an athlete can make. If the salary cap goes up, a player's value might be higher in the future.

A team has different motivations. First, it must offer enough money so that the player wants to sign. But the team doesn't want to spend too much and limit what it can pay other players. And if a contract is too long, the player might lose their skills.

This is where the negotiation comes in. Both sides present their cases for a fair contract. A contract's length and salary amount are among the hardest parts of a contract to negotiate. But determining the type of contract can be difficult too. Most sports leagues use guaranteed contracts. No matter how an athlete performs, or whether they get hurt, they will get their agreed-upon money. This is generally more beneficial to the athlete than the team.

The NFL rarely uses guaranteed contracts. NFL teams can cut players if they are underperforming or no longer fit the team's needs. In this case, any money that was not guaranteed in the contract goes away.

Quarterback Kirk Cousins is one of the few NFL players with a guaranteed contract. In 2018, he was looking for a new team.

Through the 2024 season, Kirk Cousins had earned nearly $395 million in his NFL career.

Multiple teams were ready to sign him to a major contract. One way the Minnesota Vikings set their offer apart was by offering a guaranteed contract.

The team offered Cousins the biggest contract ever at the time at three years and $84 million. And they guaranteed all of that money. When Cousins signed with the team, he became the first quarterback to have a fully guaranteed multiyear deal.

Other contracts might be smaller but full of incentives. They encourage athletes to play well and stay in shape by offering bonuses. Some of these incentives are about longevity. A player may get a bonus if they are still on the team by a certain date. Other bonuses are given when a player reaches a certain milestone. Some of these milestones can be arbitrary. But players know exactly what they need to do to get their bonuses.

During the 2024 NFL season, Tampa Bay Buccaneers wide receiver Mike Evans knew he would get a $3 million bonus if he caught at least 70 passes for at least 1,000 yards, with 10 or more touchdowns. In the last minute of the last game of the season, Evans only needed one more catch for five yards to hit that benchmark. The Buccaneers had a big lead. Normally, they would have taken a knee to run out the clock. Instead, quarterback Baker Mayfield threw the ball to Evans for a 9-yard gain to help him get his bonus.

"The conversation was . . . how do we want to formulate this play

MANNY RAMIREZ

When it comes to contracts, nothing is off-limits. Manny Ramirez's deal to play baseball in Japan is proof. When he joined the Kochi Fighting Dogs in 2017, Ramirez negotiated a list of very specific demands into his contract. One requirement was that he would receive unlimited sushi. Ramirez's contract also said he didn't have to attend practice. And a team employee had to drive him around in a Mercedes.

The 2024 NFL season was Mike Evans's 11th in a row with more than 1,000 receiving yards.

BUCCANEERS
13

CHAMPIONS
WNBA
CHAMPIONS
2024
WNBA
20 24
CHAMPIONS

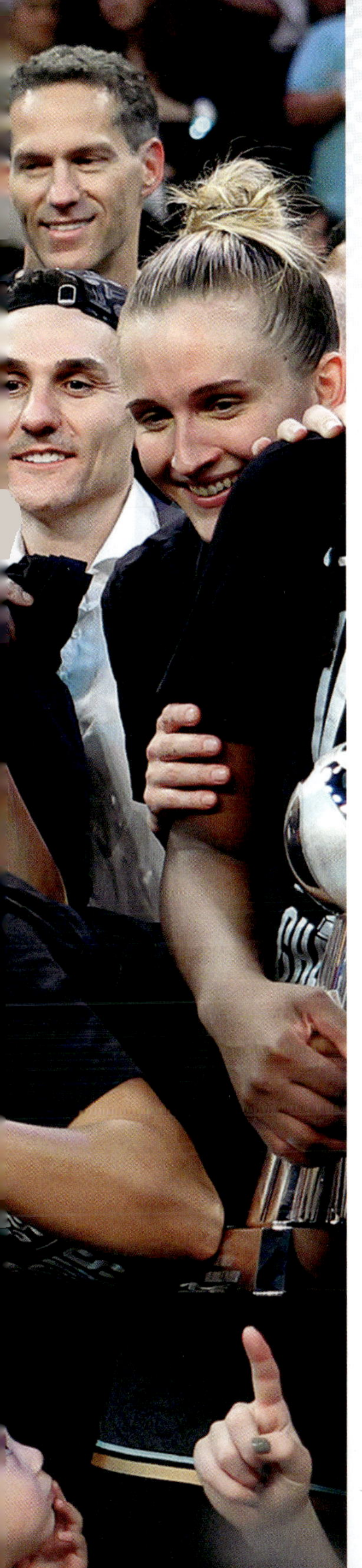

to get Mike the ball, where he can't get double-covered?" Mayfield said afterward. "That was what we came up with, and Mike did the rest."

Bonuses can also be tied to a team's performance or a player's individual awards. In the WNBA, bonuses are part of the league's rules. In 2024, every player named to the All-WNBA First Team received $10,300. And every player on the team that won the championship got $20,825.

At the end of the day, contracts are promises. For both players and team executives, contracts are about risks and rewards. They exist to help teams and athletes do the best they can. Though they might seem boring at first glance, contracts are the backbone of professional sports around the world.

The New York Liberty won the 2024 WNBA Finals.

TIMELINE

2000

The New York Mets buy out baseball player Bobby Bonilla's contract. Bonilla accepts a deferral, agreeing to receive his payments later with interest.

2007

In January, soccer midfielder David Beckham signs a five-year contract with MLS that contains a unique clause allowing him to later purchase a stake in an MLS team.

2018

In March, Kirk Cousins achieves a milestone for players in the NFL, signing the first multiyear, fully guaranteed contract by a quarterback. The contract pays $84 million over three years.

2020

In July, Kansas City Chiefs quarterback Patrick Mahomes signs the largest contract in NFL history, a 10-year deal worth $450 million.

2023

In December, baseball star Shohei Ohtani signs a free-agent contract with the Los Angeles Dodgers. The contract is worth a whopping $700 million over 10 years, making it the biggest contract in professional sports history.

2024

In December, Juan Soto agrees to a 15-year, $765 million contract with the New York Mets, breaking the record set by Ohtani the previous year.

2025

In January, English soccer team Chelsea FC pays $1.1 million to the San Diego Wave to acquire defender Naomi Girma, making Girma the first women's soccer player with a million-dollar transfer fee.

GLOSSARY

agent

A person who handles an athlete's business, including contract negotiations.

client

A person who hires someone else to work for them.

draft

A system that allows teams to acquire new players coming into a league.

endorsement

A deal in which an athlete promotes a company in exchange for the company's products or money.

free agency

A period after the season when free agents are allowed to sign with new teams.

interest

Money paid in exchange for it being borrowed.

leverage

Power in a negotiation to shape the final deal in one's favor.

retire

To end one's career.

revenue

The amount of money a company makes.

rookie

A professional athlete in their first year of competition.

signing bonus

A one-time payment that an athlete receives upon signing a contract.

MORE INFORMATION

BOOKS

Illustrated Sports Encyclopedia. DK, 2023.

McDougall, Chrös. *The Entourage: The People Behind the Athlete*. Abdo, 2026.

Rule, Heather. *Athletes as Influencers: Name, Image, and Likeness*. Abdo, 2026.

ONLINE RESOURCES

To learn more about athlete contracts and salary caps, please visit **abdobooklinks.com** or scan this QR code. These links are routinely monitored and updated to provide the most current information available.

INDEX

ABOUT THE AUTHOR

Tom Schad is an enterprise sports reporter for *USA TODAY*. He specializes in data-driven projects, human-interest stories, and coverage of sports business and legal issues. He has also covered three Olympic Games. A Colorado native and American University graduate, he previously worked at the *Commercial-Appeal* (Memphis) and the *Washington Times*.